BAKING WITHOUT SUGAR

BAKING WITHOUT SUGAR

Sophie Michell

WHITE OWL

AN IMPRINT OF PEN & SWORD BOOKS LTD.
YORKSHIRE - PHILADELPHIA

'To all my amazing family and friends who
are always there to support me'

First published in Great Britain in 2018 by PEN & SWORD WHITE OWL
An imprint of Pen & Sword Books Ltd
Yorkshire – Philadelphia

Copyright © Sophie Michell

ISBN 9781526729972

The right of Sophie Michell to be identified as Author of this work has been asserted
by her in accordance with the Copyright, Designs and Patents Act 1988.

A CIP catalogue record for this book is available from the British Library.

Printed and bound in Malta by Gutenberg Press Ltd.

Pen & Sword Books Ltd incorporates the Imprints of Aviation, Atlas, Family History,
Fiction, Maritime, Military, Discovery, Politics, History, Archaeology, Select,
Wharncliffe Local History, Wharncliffe True Crime, Military Classics, Wharncliffe
Transport, Leo Cooper, The Praetorian Press, Remember When, Seaforth Publishing
and Frontline Publishing.

For a complete list of Pen & Sword titles please contact:

PEN & SWORD BOOKS LTD
47 Church Street, Barnsley, South Yorkshire, S70 2AS, England
E-mail: enquiries@pen-and-sword.co.uk
Website: www.pen-and-sword.co.uk

or

PEN AND SWORD BOOKS
1950 Lawrence Rd, Havertown, PA 19083, USA
E-mail: Uspen-and-sword@casematepublishers.com
Website: www.penandswordbooks.com

CONTENTS

Introduction

I always seem to write books that are relevant to my life at that time. They are often created for a particular need and if that need is not being met by what's already on the market, I like to try and create it myself.

The book and TV series *Cook Yourself Thin* resonated so much with me at the time as I was in my 20s, loved my food, but also wanted to look good. *Chef on a Diet* was actually written when I was trying to slim down for my wedding, but still cooking all the time for a living; it was a diet plan for food lovers. When I am writing I tend to live, sleep, breathe and, of course, eat the book during its development. This ensures that every book is totally authentic and each recipe has been tested at least five times before publication.

I get frustrated by the lack of knowledge and honesty out there when it's linked to our health and well-being. When I was writing *Baking Without Sugar* I really was being led by my own health challenges. It was a way for me to eat sweet treats without further damaging my health, but I am getting ahead of myself, so let me explain.

About two years ago, I was diagnosed with insulin resistance and told I was pre-diabetic. Unbeknown to me this can be particularly hard on women as it affects your hormones. Half of me was relieved as it explained my little pot belly, constant fatigue, sugar cravings and inability to lose weight, but the other half of me was horrified. Did this mean I was going to get diabetes? Have you read some of the horror stories about diabetes?! Please do. Everyone should fully understand this disease which affects millions of people in the UK and the US alone, and is a massive drain on health care resources. Anyway, my doctor blithely told me to give up all carbohydrates and sugar. She also prescribed patches and gels to control my hormones, as well as the drug Metformin, which regulates your blood sugar levels.

I am someone who has eaten a high protein diet for years, but suddenly I found this stricter, more enforced regime much, much harder to deal with. I was also feeling pretty angry. Why did I have to stop eating what I wanted? I am a chef, after all! The irony was not lost on me and at first I felt like rebelling, regardless of my health. Then I calmed down and started to search for diabetes-friendly recipes and products. I was shocked to see how little choice there is and the total misinformation being fed to people. You see, the thing is, when you are trying to monitor blood sugar levels it is not just about cutting out sugar, it's about white (refined) flours, fruit, honey, agave syrup and even gluten-free flour, as they can all cause your blood sugar to spike. You can find lots of recipes with sweeteners, but then they are packed with white flour or vice versa.

Also, all the 'healthy' sweet recipes using natural sugars like honey, dates, and agave actually elevate your blood sugar levels. In fact , they are a bit of a disaster when you have diabetes and people so often don't realise that they are eating the wrong things, meaning they continue to feel ill, even when making these 'healthy' desserts and cakes. This is sometimes why the 'clean' eating movement can also be confusing; the truth is, I'm afraid, that sugar is sugar, whether it is natural or not.

So this is how I came to write a new book with classic baked goods, using ingredients that are generally gluten-free, low in sugar, with a lower GI and mostly, higher in protein. These goodies should still be enjoyed as part of a normal, healthy, balanced diet (sorry, this book is not a green light to live on sweet meals entirely; the recipes still contain calories and are still treats, but they won't damage your health as much as high sugar ones), but it does mean you can have your cake and eat it without feeling ill.

Each recipe has a code next to it and also a guideline for how easy or hard it is to make. This means you can quickly see if a particular recipe is gluten-free, for example. I do use spelt flour

Gluten-free

Diabetic friendly

in some of the recipes, and although it's not gluten-free, it does release the energy into your bloodstream more slowly, and a lot of people with wheat intolerance find it easier to digest. You can also check whether a particular recipe is 'diabetic friendly' and dairy-free too. These recipes are for everyone, you don't need to have diabetes to benefit from cutting down on sugar because, after all, more and more health experts are telling us that it is sugar that is affecting our health far more than fat. If you are dieting, most of the recipes are lower carb and paleo-friendly, so are perfect for helping you on your path to a slimmer you.

I have used sweeteners in all of these recipes. Luckily, we can now access natural sweeteners like *Xylitol*, *Stevia* and *Erythritol*, which unlike the old aspartame-based sweeteners, don't come with any unhealthy side effects. Of course, some people don't believe that sweeteners are very good for you, but there's absolutely ZERO research to show that they are bad for your health.

It is all down to personal choice, though. I know that sugar is a bigger health threat to me and my body than sweeteners, and I am happy to bake with them so that I can keep eating fantastic food. Personally, I believe that when eaten as part of a balanced diet, sweeteners are frankly amazing, and I have learned so much from practising with them. However, you can substitute with natural sugar if you prefer – it's your choice!

Don't be alarmed by the strange names of the sweeteners. I have listed them with their basic names, but there are various brands available in supermarkets that you can use, and to be honest, they are all pretty much interchangeable. However, some can taste sweeter than others, but don't lose sleep over it and keep on cooking.

It was really important to me that these recipes tasted and felt like their sugar-filled counterparts. I don't want a healthy tasting carrot cake, I want one that tastes totally full of sugar like it's been bought in a shop, and a muffin just like the one I would get with my coffee in the local café. I feel I have achieved this with the recipes.

My husband and I even did a taste test on our friends, and it was always difficult for them to tell the difference.

I find it interesting that even though I feel like I am having a 'normal' dessert or pudding when I eat the treats from this book, I never get the heady sugar rush, headaches and fatigue that I used to experience after eating sugar-laden treats. My health is an onward journey; sometimes it's great, sometimes it's not. I do know that the only thing that makes a difference is truly looking after myself and being conscious of my actions and diet, something that the hard-working, hard-partying chef in me has taken years to acknowledge. I hope you love my recipes too and that they become part of you and your family's meals.

I will continue to write new recipes and post them on social media channels, so please join me on my journey and contact me with your questions and comments. The ingredients we use for these recipes are less standardised than normal flour and sugar, so feel free to reach out to me and I will help as much as possible. We are in this together and let's try to aim for long-lasting, optimum health!

love, sophie xxx

Twitter @sophiemichell
Instagram @sophiemichell

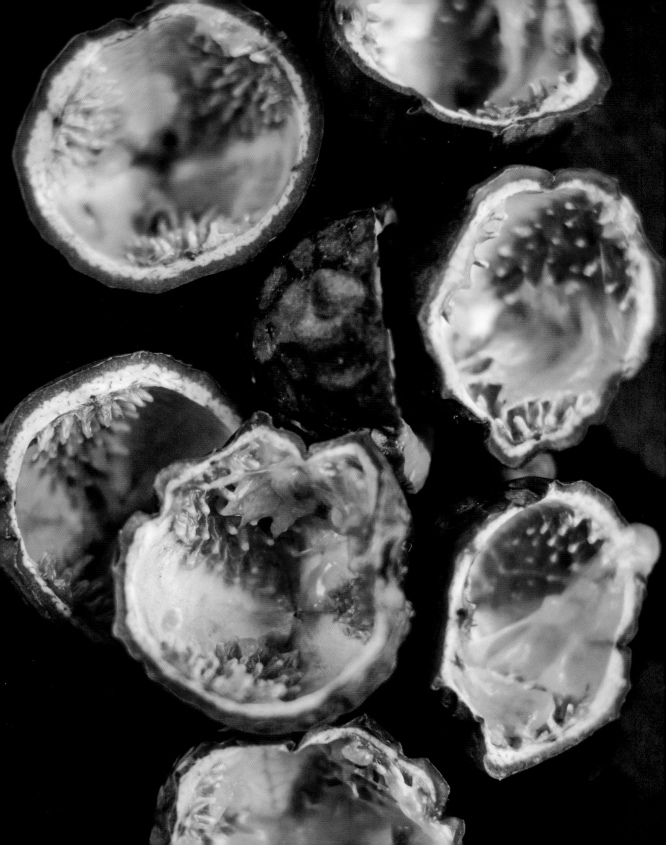

CAKES

CARROT CAKE

This is one of those classic cakes that everyone should have a good recipe for. I never get bored of the moist cinnamon, carrot sponge and whipped creamy frosting. It was the first sugar-free cake that I experimented with and it inspired me to write this book, so it's a good one for you all to start with too!

100g coconut flour
150g almond flour
200g *Xylitol*
2 tsp baking powder
1 tsp bicarb of soda
2 tbsp cinnamon
1 tsp mixed spice
6 medium eggs
300ml milk
200g melted butter
1 tsp vanilla extract
250g carrots, grated
1 medium apple, grated

Icing
800g cream cheese
50g *Xylitol* icing sugar
50ml maple syrup
1 tsp cinnamon

Preheat the oven to 160C/gas mark 3. Grease and line the base of two 9-inch springform cake tins. Mix all the dry ingredients together in a large bowl, then in a separate bowl, whisk the eggs, butter, vanilla extract and milk.

Peel and grate the carrot on a coarse grater, along with the apple (no need to peel either), then add to the egg mix and stir until combined. Finally, fold in the flour mix and stir well. Divide the mix between the two tins and bake for 40 minutes until a skewer comes out clean and the cake is slightly raised and golden, then take out of the oven and cool completely.

While it is cooling, you can make the icing. Sift the icing sugar and then mix well with the cream cheese, maple syrup and cinnamon. When you are ready, spread a generous layer of cream cheese frosting on the first half of the cake, place the second layer on top and then add a layer of frosting. Sprinkle with cinnamon and serve.

PISTACHIO CAKE WITH ROSEWATER ICING

SERVES 6

This is the ultimate pretty party cake. I love the flavours of pistachio and rose together, and the greens and pinks make me incredibly happy. This is a time where I get out my vintage crockery and go to town. I have inherited lots of beautiful china (including the ones in the picture) and I love to bring them out and think of years of my family enjoying them.

Butter or vegetable oil, for greasing
300g pistachios
4 tbsp *Xylitol*
8 free-range egg whites

Filling
200ml double cream
1 tsp vanilla extract

Icing
200g *Xylitol* icing sugar
1 tsp rosewater
splash of water to get to icing consistency
(rose petals and pistachios to decorate)

Preheat the oven to 160C/gas mark 3. Grease and line a 5/6-inch cake tin. Blitz the pistachios and half the *Xylitol* in a blender until fine and powdery. Whisk the egg whites until they form soft peaks and then gently, one spoonful at a time, with whisking in between, add the remaining *Xylitol* and whisk until stiff. Then fold in the powdered nut mix and mix well.

Pour into the cake tin and bake for 30 minutes, then cool. When cooled completely, whisk the double cream and vanilla together to form soft peaks. Slice the cake VERY carefully horizontally across into three layers (it is extremely delicate, so please be gentle). Spread half of the cream mix on the bottom layer, then place another layer of cake and cream, and place the final cake layer on top. To make the icing, whisk the icing sugar, rosewater and water together, then drizzle over the cake and decorate with rose petals and pistachios.

CHOCOLATE CAKE

SERVES 8

Chocolate cake is one of those dishes that I could not think about making without sugar and gluten, as it really represents indulgence to me. I wanted this to be a really normal chocolate sponge cake with the kind of frosting you get in cake stores, and it worked! I know there is some sugar in chocolate, but if you stick to good quality dark chocolate with high cocoa solids, it's not much, and you benefit from all those antioxidants too.

100g cocoa
50g cup coconut flour
3 tsp baking powder
Pinch of salt
6 eggs
125g *Xylitol*
75g melted butter
180ml soured cream
1 tsp vanilla paste

Frosting
200g dark chocolate
100g butter
200g cream cheese
150g *Xylitol* icing sugar
2 tbsp cocoa powder
1 tsp vanilla extract
150ml double cream

This is such a simple cake! Preheat the oven to 160C/ gas mark 3, then line and grease an 8-inch cake tin. Mix all the dried ingredients together in one bowl, then all the wet in another. Combine and mix well. Bake for 45-50 minutes and then cool.

While this is cooking, you can make the frosting. Add the butter and chocolate to a small saucepan and very slowly, on a low heat, melt (you can also do this in a bowl over simmering water if you are worried about it splitting or burning). Then sift the cocoa and icing sugar into a large mixing bowl, add and combine the cream cheese and vanilla, and mix well. Finally, add the melted chocolate and butter and the double cream. Mix carefully.

When cooled, carefully cut horizontally across into two, then spread the chocolate frosting on the bottom layer. Place the top back on and then spread a thick layer of frosting on top. Chill and then serve.

MANDARIN, ROSEMARY, OLIVE OIL AND ALMOND CAKE

SERVES 8–10

This is already a classic Mediterranean recipe that I haven't really adapted much past adding the rosemary and olive oil. My family lives in Greece and this reminds me of the cakes we get there. It will bring a little bit of sunshine to your day too. I generally don't like massively sweet cakes and this is the perfect breakfast cake with some Greek style yoghurt.

3 mandarins
6 eggs
200g *Xylitol*
250g ground almonds
100ml extra virgin olive oil
1 tsp baking powder
1 handful flaked almonds
1 sprig rosemary

Put the mandarins in a pan with some cold water, bring to the boil and cook for two hours. Don't forget to keep covering them in water, as they can boil dry. When the two hours are up, drain off and cool. When cooled, cut each mandarin in half and remove the pips. Then place the mandarins – skins, pith, fruit and all – into a blender and give a quick blitz into a relatively smooth puree. Preheat the oven to 190C/ gas mark 5. Oil and line a 21cm/ 8-inch springform tin.

Beat the eggs and oil together and add the *Xylitol*, almonds and baking powder, and finally the pulped mandarins.

Place the sprig of rosemary in the bottom of the lined tin; the rosemary will add a delicate flavour. Pour the cake mixture into the tin and bake for an hour, when a skewer should come out clean; you'll probably have to cover with foil or greaseproof paper after about 40 minutes to stop the top burning. Remove from the oven and, leaving it in the tin, place on a rack to cool. When completely cooled, turn upside down, take out of the tin, sprinkle with some flaked almonds and serve with Greek yoghurt.

EARL GREY CHAI MUFFIN BITES

MAKES ABOUT 24

DF

This is possibly one of my favourite recipes in the book as the aromatic combination of the infused Earl Grey, spices and soft spelt sponge is a winner. I have kept nearly all the recipes gluten-free, but spelt is such a good flour to cook with that I couldn't help but add a few recipes using it. Spelt flour is great for diabetics (as it is slow releasing and has a low GI) and a lot of people who are wheat intolerant can process it too. I have used wholemeal here, as it makes it even better for you, but the white spelt flour is fabulous in sauces and baking too. If you do have an intolerance to wheat, then sampling this is all about trial and error, so listen to what your body is telling you and introduce it slowly.

450ml full fat milk
2 Earl Grey teabags
4 cardamom pods, squashed
200g wholemeal spelt flour
200g *Xylitol*
1 tsp baking powder
1 tsp bicarb of soda
1 tsp salt
1 tsp cinnamon
1 tsp mixed spice
½ tsp ground cloves
½ tsp freshly grated nutmeg
½ tsp turmeric
1 egg
¼ cup vegetable oil
100g butter (softened for
    greasing the mini muffin trays)

Spiced sugar
200g *Xylitol*
1 tsp cinnamon
1 tsp mixed spices

Preheat the oven to 180C/gas mark 4 and soften the butter. To get started, infuse the milk by pouring it into a small saucepan, adding the tea bags and cardamom, then slowly bringing to just below boil on a medium heat. It will take about 8-10 minutes. Take it off the heat and leave to cool. Mix all the dried ingredients together in a large bowl, then in a separate bowl mix the infused milk, egg and vegetable oil together and then whisk into the dry mix.

Take two small muffin tins and line generously with softened butter, then spoon a dessert spoonful in each muffin indentation. Bake for 10 minutes until risen and spongy, then take out and cool. Finally, blitz the spices and sugar together until fine and then sprinkle over while still warm. Serve warm or cool, and keep in an airtight container once cooled.

BUCKWHEAT, CHESTNUT CRÊPE CAKE

SERVES 10–12

This cake is a real showstopper, but I am not going to lie, it takes time – a lot of time. You need to make 30 crêpes, but it can be quite therapeutic and once you get into the swing of it, you can do it easily. It's a good one for Christmas – get your family to keep you company and make it an occasion in itself.

Buckwheat pancakes
1kg buckwheat flour
1 tsp salt
3 eggs
1L milk
600ml water
150g melted butter

Chestnut mix
500g unsweetened
    chestnut puree
100g *Xylitol*
100ml double cream
25ml maple syrup
1 tsp vanilla extract

Whipped cream
2 tbsp brandy (optional)
500ml double cream
1 tsp vanilla seeds from a
    pod or good quality
    paste
Persimmon, cape
    gooseberries and gold
    leaf to decorate

Firstly mix the buckwheat flour and salt together in a large bowl. Then mix the eggs, milk, water and melted butter together in another. Carefully pour the liquids into the dry mix and whisk well to combine without any lumps, and then let the batter sit for 30 minutes. Using a pancake or crêpe pan (preferably non-stick) make about 30 pancakes. The best method for this is to heat the pan up super hot, add about 2 tablespoons of neutral (non-flavoured) oil, and some butter, and drain the excess off in a small heatproof container by the stove, keeping just enough to grease the bottom of the pan.

Using a large ladle, scoop up the batter, filling the ladle about two-thirds full. Then spoon into the pan, quickly swirl around to cover and use a small palette knife to spread more. Cook for a few minutes, and then flip over. I know this takes ages, but try to enjoy the process; it is worth it. Why not rope someone in to hang out and chat with you while you do it? You can make the crêpes up to two days ahead and then assemble on the actual day.

Keep the crêpes piled up on a plate and then start on the filling. For the chestnut layer, beat the chestnut puree with the vanilla, sweetener, cream and maple syrup, and then set aside. Then whip the cream and the vanilla up to soft peaks in a separate bowl. When they are both ready you can start to layer up the cake. I do crêpe, chestnut puree, then crêpe, then cream, and repeat 30 times. Spread thinly and evenly, so when you cut into it you have lots of beautiful equal layers. When you get to the top, add another layer of cream, and then decorate with sliced persimmon and cape gooseberries.

BISCUITS, BARS AND PANCAKES

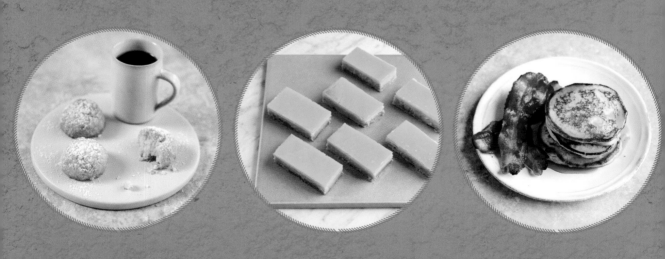

MILLIONAIRE'S SHORTBREAD

MAKES 12–15

Millionaire's shortbread is a classic sweet that my grandma used to make for me when I spent time with her in Cheshire, so it is a firm favourite of mine. Since being diagnosed with insulin resistance it's been off my list of allowed foods, so I was delighted to develop this recipe.

Shortbread
150g coconut flour
50g of *Xylitol*
150g butter
pinch of salt

Caramel
300g smooth almond butter
     (wholegrain)
100g maple syrup
200g brown sweetener (*Sukrin*
     is good)
250g cup coconut oil, melted
1 tsp vanilla extract
Pinch of salt

Chocolate topping
100ml coconut oil, melted
100g cup dark chocolate, melted
Sea salt flakes

Preheat the oven to 180C/gas mark 4. Grease a 14 x 5-inch pan and line with baking paper. Mix the coconut flour, *Xylitol* and salt in a bowl. Melt the butter, mix into the flour and shape into a dough. Place the dough into the tin as level as possible, press down to be smooth. Bake for 10 minutes and then cool.

For the filling, mix all the ingredients together in a pan, heat until they are combined well and then pour over the shortbread base. Cool completely and allow to set in the fridge before adding the caramel layer.

For the topping, mix all the ingredients in another small pan and gently warm through until the chocolate is melted. Pour over the chilled caramel and sprinkle with the sea salt flakes. Then pop back in the fridge until set and cut into fingers or squares when ready to serve. I keep this in the fridge as the caramel can get soft when it warms up.

RASPBERRY AND ALMOND TRAYBAKE

MAKES 14 SLICES

*The smell of freshly baked frangipane (the classic French almond sponge)
coming out of the oven is amazing. This is a bake that needs to be cooled
completely before you eat it. It will keep for a week or so in an airtight
container kept in a cool place, and is good for school lunches and snacks too.
It also works with all sorts of fruit, so is a fantastic seasonal bake. I make it
with plums in autumn, rhubarb in winter, and strawberries or blueberries
in summer.*

200g butter
100g *Xylitol*
4 drops *Stevia*
270g almond flour
1 tsp gluten-free baking powder
4 eggs
1 tsp almond extract
250g raspberries
1 tbsp *Xylitol* icing sugar

Preheat the oven to 160C/gas mark 3. Grease and line
a tin of approximately 6 x 11 - inches. Take a medium
sized bowl, beat together the butter and *Xylitol*
until well combined and light in colour (this should
take about 5-8 minutes by hand). Then gradually
add the eggs one by one, *Stevia* drops and almond
extract, scraping the sides down in between to mix
thoroughly. Mix the almond flour and baking powder
together, and then fold into the egg and butter mix.
Stir in well and then spoon into the baking tray.
Spread and smooth out and then press in all the
raspberries.

Bake for 40-50 minutes or until golden and cooked
through. Don't worry that its appearance isn't firm at
this stage. Then take out of the oven, cool completely
and dust with the icing sugar. Serve with clotted
cream if desired.

PROTEIN RICOTTA PANCAKES WITH STREAKY BACON AND SMOKED MAPLE SYRUP

SERVES 4

Pancakes used to be my favourite breakfast, but they would make my blood sugar spike and crash so much that I had to stop eating them. I used to especially love the big fluffy ones served in the US with masses of maple syrup and bacon. Well, here are some that you can eat without feeling you're doing yourself any damage. Yes, the maple syrup is a sugar, but it has a lower GI than white sugar, and the bacon, ricotta and eggs add valuable protein to slow down the insulin reaction.

250g ricotta
25g coconut flour
2 eggs (separated)
1 tsp *Xylitol*
1 tsp vanilla extract
100ml milk
4 rashers of streaky bacon
3 tbsp maple syrup
150g butter
1 tsp smoked sea salt
½ tsp Espelette chilli pepper
    flakes

Firstly, make the chilli maple butter. I like to have this in my fridge or freezer to bring out for pancakes when needed. Basically you just soften the butter, then beat it together with the maple syrup, chilli flakes and smoked salt. You can roll it into a sausage, wrap in cling film and slice when you need it.

Mix the ricotta, coconut flour, *Xylitol*, vanilla and egg yolks together. Then add the milk and whisk well. In a separate bowl, whisk the egg whites until they make soft peaks and then fold into the batter. Heat the grill up high and place the bacon on a tray and then under the grill and cook until crisp and golden, then keep warm in a low oven.

Heat a non-stick frying pan to a medium heat, add a splash of oil and then add two large dessert spoonfuls of mixture for each pancake into the pan, and cook for 3 minutes on each side, until golden brown. You can probably fit about four in the pan at the same time. Keep them warm in the oven and continue to cook all the mix. Then serve with the streaky bacon, some melted chilli maple butter and some extra maple syrup if desired.

AMARETTI BISCUITS

MAKES 10–12

Amaretti biscuits are such a classic and so easy to make. They are the perfect accompaniment to a strong coffee mid-morning and the joy is that you are actually having a protein ball, full of good fats, even though it tastes super indulgent. I still can't believe I am eating sugar-free, high protein goodies with this recipe; it's only when I don't get the crazy highs and lows of the sugar hit that I truly appreciate their goodness.

2 large egg whites
200g ground almonds
½ tsp almond essence
1 tbsp amaretto
150g *Xylitol*
50g *Xylitol* icing sugar

Preheat the oven to 150C/gas mark 2. Then line a baking sheet with baking paper. Add the ground almonds to a bowl and add the almond essence. Whisk the egg whites to stiff peaks and fold into the almond mix. Combine well and then add the amaretto liqueur. Take about a dessert spoon of the mix, roll into a ball then roll in the icing sugar. Place on the tray and bake for 20 minutes, until the biscuits start to puff up and crack. Remove from the oven, cool and serve.

LEMON BARS

These fragrant lemon bars are wonderful eaten on the day they are made, to get the real zingy lemon hit. They have corn starch in so have a slightly higher GI rating than some recipes here, but this is still relatively low compared to most normal sweets. You can also experiment with flavours too; try them with lime juice and zest, grapefruit, blood orange or even passionfruit.

150g coconut flour
100g cashew butter
125g butter
Juice of ½ lemon
Zest of 1 lemon
1 tsp vanilla extract
Zest of 2 lemons and juice of
    6 lemons
200g *Xylitol*
6 eggs
3 tbsps corn starch
Powdered sweetner to dust

Preheat the oven to 180C/gas mark 4. Then mix the coconut flour, cashew butter, butter, lemon zest, juice and vanilla together. Next line a baking tray with baking paper and carefully press the mix into the bottom, spread it as evenly as possible and prick with a fork. Cook for about 15 minutes until golden and cooked through. Then turn the oven down to 160C/gas mark 3, take the tray out and cool completely.

For the filling, take a large bowl and whisk together the lemon zest, juice, sweetener, eggs and corn starch until well combined and lump free. Then pour the mix carefully over the base and pop back in the oven for 20 minutes or until just set and a little wobbly. Take out and cool completely before cutting into bars. Finally, sprinkle with powdered sweetner.

CHOCOLATE CHIP COOKIES

MAKES 12

Chocolate chip cookies are a staple in most houses and this recipe really is a quick everyday treat you can rustle up. The chocolate does contain low amounts of sugar, but always use dark, as it has a lower GI, is full of antioxidants and the flavour goes a long way. You can also add chopped nuts to this recipe for added protein.

150g ground almonds
½ tsp baking powder
100ml of milk
1 egg
100g butter
50g *Xylitol* (brown)
1 tsp vanilla extract
50g dark chocolate chips

Preheat the oven to 180C/gas mark 4. Mix all the ingredients together and then spoon in dollops on to a greased and lined baking tray. Bake for 15 minutes until the biscuits are starting to get golden around the edges and then cool and eat. Yes, it's that simple!!

NUT BUTTER COOKIES

All of the cookies below are quick fix nibbles, using nut butters as a base. You simply beat them together and that's it. I have tried a few variations and these are my favourites.

PEANUT COOKIES
MAKES 8–10
200g peanut butter
Pinch of sea salt
1 egg
100g *Xylitol*
1 tbsp of chocolate chips

Preheat the oven to 180C/gas mark 4. Line a baking sheet. Mix all the ingredients together and then take about a dessert spoon of the mix and roll into a ball. Press down into the palm of your hand and then place it on the baking sheet. Press down with a fork and bake for about 15 minutes. The longer you bake them the crisper and crunchier they get. With less cooking time, they are fudgier.

GINGER SNAPS
MAKES 8–10
200g cashew butter
1 egg
100g *Xylitol*
1 tsp mixed spice
1 tsp ground ginger

Follow the exact same baking instructions as for the the peanut cookies.

LEMON AND MACADAMIA
200g cashew butter
Zest of 1 lemon
1 egg
100g *Xylitol*
50g chopped macadamia nuts

Again, follow the same baking instructions.

OAT, BANANA AND CINNAMON COOKIES

MAKES 8–10

These have a higher GI than the previous cookie recipes, but the large, gluten-free oats are slow energy releasing and combined with the protein nut butter and the banana they are a great energy boost for children.

2 ripe bananas, smashed
150g large gluten-free oats
50g brown *Xylitol*
100g of cashew butter
1 tsp cinnamon

Preheat the oven to 180C/gas mark 4. Line a baking sheet. Mash up the banana and then mix all the ingredients together. Take a dessert spoonful of the mix and roll into a ball. Press down into the palm of your hand and place on the baking sheet and cook for about 15-20 minutes until golden brown and then serve.

PUDDINGS AND PIES

BANANA CRÈME PIE

SERVES 8

What a classic! This is childhood comfort food at its best, and there is something about banana, cream and custard that makes me happy. You can make the tart case and fill it the day before, then add the bananas and cream on the day you are planning to eat it – perfect!

6 ripe bananas
400ml double cream
1 tsp vanilla extract

Custard
4 egg yolks
500ml milk
100g *Xylitol*
½ tsp vanilla extract
4 tbsp cornflour
Pinch of salt

Tart case
(see shortcrust recipe on p.88)

Preheat the oven to 180C/gas mark 4. Make the pastry and blind bake the tart case.

To make the custard, whisk the egg yolks together in a medium bowl. Then mix the milk, cornflour, sweetener, vanilla and salt together in a saucepan. Place on a medium heat and then slowly bring to just below boiling. Pour half the milk mix on to the eggs and whisk well, then strain the mix back in the remaining milk and into the saucepan. Continue to heat gently until the mixture is bubbling and thickened. Then take off the heat, pour into a bowl and cover with cling film, and place on top of a larger bowl filled with ice.

When cooled, whisk to remove any lumps, then pour the custard into the pastry case, spread and smooth over. Take the bananas and slice thinly, layering the slices on top of the custard. Then whip the cream and the vanilla together and spread over the top. Chill for 15 minutes and serve.

BOURBON ROASTED PEACH CHEESECAKE PIE

SERVES 8

Peaches are such a wonderful summer treat and they make me think of balmy warm evenings and simple, pretty desserts. This pudding makes a lovely end to a meal and you can replace the peaches with whatever you have at hand; think raspberries, apricots, plums or even strawberries. It's a great base for many different seasonal fruits.

1 batch of shortcrust pastry
4 white peaches
1 tbsp bourbon (optional)
1 tbsp *Xylitol* sweetener
50g butter
250g cream cheese
150g *Xylitol*
2 eggs
100ml double cream
1 vanilla pod, seeds scraped in
Juice from half a lemon

Preheat the oven to 180C/gas mark 4. Make the pastry and blind bake the tart case. At the same time, you can roast the peaches. Simply cut into quarters, remove the stones and place in an even layer in a roasting tray, and then sprinkle with the bourbon, sweetener and dot with butter. Roast for about 20 minutes until softened. Then take out of the oven and cool slightly.

When the tart case is cool, add a layer of the peaches to the bottom. Beat the cream cheese and *Xylitol* together, then add the eggs one by one, beating until smooth, and then add the cream, vanilla seeds and lemon juice. Pour this mix over the peaches in the tart case and bake in a 160C oven for 20 minutes, then take out, cool and serve.

PEANUT BUTTER PIE

SERVES 8

This is one of the easiest recipes in this book. Peanut butter is a wonderful ingredient for sugar-free baking. Try to get a good quality make though, as the types of oil they are made with vary hugely and you may want to avoid palm oil.

One batch of chocolate
    pastry (p.88)

Peanut butter filling
550g cream cheese
300g smooth peanut butter
100g *Xylitol*
Pinch of salt
½ tsp vanilla extract

Caramel nut topping
400g of brown *Xylitol*
75ml water
½ tsp sea salt
300g raw, unsalted peanuts

Preheat the oven to 180C/gas mark 4. Make the pastry and blind bake the tart case. Take out of the oven and cool completely.

To make the filling, just beat all the ingredients together, then spoon into the tart case and spread smoothly. Chill for a few hours before serving.

An hour or so before serving you can make the caramel. Simply add the sweetener and water to a pan and bring to the boil, then turn down and simmer until thick, and then add the peanuts and salt. Cool slightly and when ready to eat, spoon over some of the peanuts and serve with whipped cream.

PUMPKIN PIE

SERVES 8

The ultimate dessert for autumn and the festive season. It works really well as a sugar-free recipe, as the pumpkin adds sweetness and moisture to everything. I have this on my restaurant menu and everyone loves it, and at Thanksgiving, we even serve it with sugar-free eggnog cream. It tastes really indulgent.

Spice 'shortcrust' pastry
2 eggs
½ tsp sea salt
120g coconut flour
1tsp mixed spice
150g cold butter, cubed

Filling
200g sweetener
1 tbsp cornflour
2 tsp cinnamon
½ tsp ground ginger
A grating of nutmeg
¼ tsp ground cloves
1 tsp vanilla extract
Pinch of salt
1 tin pumpkin puree
¾ cup double cream
½ cup sour cream
3 eggs

Preheat the oven to 180C/gas mark 4. First bake the pastry. To make the pastry, add the butter, coconut flour, mixed spice and sea salt to a mixer bowl and mix until it resembles breadcrumbs. Then whisk the eggs and add to the mix. Continue mixing until a crumbly dough is formed, and take this out of the mixer and roll out between two baking paper sheets. Press into a pie or tart dish, prick with a fork and then blind bake for 20 minutes.

Remove the pastry base from the oven, cool slightly and reduce the oven to 150C/gas mark 2. For the filling, simply mix the pumpkin puree, spices, cornflour, vanilla extract and sweetener together and then whisk in the eggs and cream. Mix well and pour into the tart case and bake for 30 minutes until just set. Cool and serve with whipped cream.

CINNAMON, SPELT AND APPLE CRUMBLE WITH CLOTTED CREAM

SERVES 4

This had to be included. It does contain spelt flour, so it is not gluten-free I'm afraid, but I find spelt flour doesn't have the same effect as refined white flour on my energy levels and digestion, so if you want a healthier crumble, with slow-releasing energy, this is the one for you. It's a really good one for children too.

250g spelt flour
125g brown *Xylitol*
1 tsp of salt
125g cold butter, cubed
100g old-fashioned oats
    (larger and not rolled)

Filling
400g cooking apples
100g sultanas
100g brown *Xylitol*
50ml water
2 tsp cinnamon
50g butter

Preheat the oven to 180C/gas mark 4. Make the apple filling by just peeling, coring and chopping the apples up roughly. Add them to a saucepan along with the sultanas, *Xylitol*, butter, water and cinnamon, bring up to the boil, then turn down and simmer for 15 minutes, until softened.

In a large bowl mix the spelt flour, *Xylitol,* oats and salt together. Next add the cold butter and start rubbing it into the dry ingredients. You want to get some height and rub with your fingers, until it resembles fine breadcrumbs.

Spread the stewed apple mix in a baking dish about 5 x 7 inches and then sprinkle the crumbled flour mix over the top. Bake for 30/40 minutes.

I love this with Greek yoghurt, but if you are not too worried about the sugar content, the maple syrup custard on page 62 is lovely.

MACADAMIA NUT CHEESECAKE WITH CHARGRILLED PINEAPPLE

SERVES 8

Baked cheesecakes are so popular and really work with a nut base. I have gone for a classic vanilla cream one here, but when you get the base right you can experiment with all sorts of flavours. Macadamia nuts are really buttery and taste very indulgent, and I love them for snacking on too. I have finished this one off with a pineapple salsa for a slightly tropical feel, but it's great without too.

50g butter, softened, plus extra
    for greasing
500g cream cheese, softened
1 tbsp cornflour
200g sweetener
4 drops of *Stevia*
1 vanilla pod
3 eggs
200ml double cream
1 tsp lemon juice

Macadamia nut crust
300g macadamia nuts
100g brown *Xylitol*
100g desiccated coconut
Pinch of sea salt
100g Butter

To serve
1 small pineapple
1 lime zest and juice

Preheat the oven to 180C/gas mark 4. Mix the macadamia nuts, coconut, brown *Xylitol* and salt together and then blitz to breadcrumb consistency. Line a 9-inch tin with baking paper and then press the nut mix into the bottom. Bake in the oven for 15-20 minutes until golden and set. Take out and cool. Then take a large bowl and combine the cream cheese, butter, cornflour and sweetener together until smooth. Add the eggs one by one, beating in between, then finally add the cream, vanilla and lemon juice.

Pour the mix into the cake tin and wrap the OUTSIDE of the tin with foil. Place into a deep baking or roasting tray and pour hot water in around the tray and place in the oven. Bake for 40 minutes until set and golden. Then take out of the oven and the pan of water, and cool completely. I tend to make this cake a day before eating.

For the topping, trim the top and bottom off the pineapple and the skin and spiky part. Cut into slices and chargrill or pan fry on both sides until it is golden and caramelised. Then take off the heat and cool, dice into small squares, add the lime zest and juice. Stir well and leave to sit for 30 minutes. Cut the cheesecake into slices and serve with the salsa.

CINNAMON SWIRL MINI CHEESECAKES

MAKES 12

Who doesn't like the flavour of cinnamon? I love cinnamon buns, but they really hit me with the white sugar and refined flour. However, these little handheld darlings are packed with protein and are the perfect sweet treat for those of you who carefully monitor your portions. They are great for packed lunches too.

50g butter, softened, plus extra
    for greasing
500g cream cheese, softened
1 tbsp cornflour
100g *Xylitol* sweetener,
    granulated
2 drops of *Stevia*
1 vanilla pod
3 eggs
200ml double cream
1 tsp lemon juice

Crust
100g butter, melted
200g almond flour
2 tbsp *Xylitol*, granulated
1 tsp cinnamon

Cinnamon syrup
1 tbsp cinnamon
150g *Xylitol*, granulated
50ml water

For the crust, mix the almond flour, *Xylitol*, cinnamon and butter together. Then press into the holes in a muffin tin and chill in the fridge. Preheat the oven to 160C/gas mark 3. To make the cinnamon syrup, add all of the ingredients to a small saucepan and bring to the boil and simmer for 10 minutes, before chilling. Then mix the butter, cream cheese, cornflour, *Xylitol*, *Stevia* and vanilla pod seeds, and beat until smooth. Next gradually whisk the eggs in one at a time, and then the double cream. Finally, mix in the lemon juice. Pour or spoon the mixture into each muffin hole, add half a teaspoon of the cinnamon syrup, and swirl round to each mould. Bake for 10 minutes then chill. Carefully take out of the moulds with a small knife and serve. Great as protein-packed snacks.

BUTTERMILK PANNA COTTA WITH BLUEBERRY COMPOTE

SERVES 4

Panna cottas are so easy to do sugar-free, and I always think they are a pretty impressive dessert for when you have friends over. Again, you can experiment with flavours, but you can't beat blueberry and vanilla. The buttermilk adds a slight tanginess to it that I think works really well. I also make this with roasted apricots and peaches when in season.

3 gelatine leaves
400ml double cream
400ml buttermilk
200g *Xylitol*

Compote
400g blueberries
50g *Xylitol*
1 tsp vanilla extract

Soak the gelatine leaves in cold water. Then heat the double cream and *Xylitol* in a saucepan until the sugar has dissolved. Take it off the heat, squeeze the water out of the gelatine leaves and add them to the cream. Stir well until dissolved, and then mix in the buttermilk until completely combined.

Pour the mix into panna cotta moulds and then pop them in the fridge to chill and set. This should take a few hours. While they are chilling, you can make the compote. To do this, add the blueberries, *Xylitol* and vanilla to a small saucepan, bring to the boil, then turn down and simmer for 10 minutes. Cool completely.

When you are ready to eat, place the panna cotta moulds on to your serving plate or bowl and blowtorch the top and sides of the mould. Carefully ease the panna cottas out and spoon some of the compote around them.

STICKY TOFFEE AND BANANA PUDDING WITH MAPLE SYRUP CUSTARD

SERVES 6

We have epic Sunday lunches at home and it is my favourite time of the week – perfect for having friends over and really relaxing. Often two guests end up being fifteen and everyone hangs out all afternoon, chatting, eating and drinking. We usually do two types of meat, such as a slow-roasted pork with apple, and a leg of lamb with garlic and rosemary. This is accompanied by four vegetable dishes, which tend to be roast carrots or parsnips with mustard, truffle cauliflower cheese, peas with leeks, red cabbage and duck fat 'roasties'. Then we have a pudding as well, which is always the highlight of the meal, and none of our guests EVER guess this is low in sugar. I serve it with a jug of home-made custard and a touch of maple syrup.

100g dates
200ml boiling water
100g butter
200g almond flour
1 tbsp coconut flour
100g brown *Xylitol*
4 bananas
1 tsp sea salt
1 tsp bicarb of soda

Maple syrup custard
4 egg yolks
1 tbsp cornflour
250ml cream
250ml milk
1 split vanilla pod
1 tbsp maple syrup

Chop the dates up and place in a bowl, then pour over the boiling water and add the butter. In a separate bowl, mix the almond flour, coconut flour, *Xylitol*, sea salt and bicarb. Then blitz 3 bananas to a puree and mix with the eggs. Add all this to the other bowl containing the dates.

Grease a baking dish (9 x 5 inches) with some butter and then pour in the batter. Slice the remaining banana lengthways and then lay on top. Bake for 40 minutes at 180C/gas mark 4.

While the pudding is cooking, you can start on the custard. Heat the milk and cream with the vanilla pod. Bring it to just boiling. Then place the egg yolks, maple syrup and cornflour in a mixing bowl and whisk well.

When the milk is hot, pour on to the egg mix and whisk well before pouring back into the saucepan. Slowly increase the heat and keep stirring until the custard is thickened. When it is thick enough to coat the back of a spoon, take off the heat, and it is ready to serve.

PEANUT BUTTER FONDANTS

MAKES 4

These are easy to make, and unbelievably impressive, but the timing of the cooking is UBER important. I would say practice makes perfect so you can get a feel for when they are ready. This is a great excuse for you to eat a few extra in the name of perfecting the recipe and then you can impress your friends and family later down the line. You want them cooked enough on the outside to hold shape, but still molten inside. Also, greasing the moulds is very important!

100g butter (plus 50g for
   greasing)
25g cocoa powder
100g chocolate
100g *Xylitol*
1 egg yolk
1 whole egg
3 tbsp almond flour
1 tsp vanilla extract
Pinch of sea salt
4 large dessert spoons of
   peanut butter

Soften the butter for greasing and brush a thick layer inside each mould, then chill and repeat. After the second layer of butter, instead of placing in the fridge, dust the inside with cocoa powder. Then set aside.

Preheat the oven to 180C/gas mark 4. You can make the pudding mix an hour or so before cooking, but you need to bake them just before serving.

Melt the 100g butter and chocolate together in a bowl over a pan of simmering water. Whisk the *Xylitol* egg and egg yolk together until light and fluffy, then fold in the dry ingredients. Spoon the batter mix about halfway up each mould, add a spoonful of peanut butter to each, and then fill with more batter. Bake for 20 minutes, then turn them out on to a plate.

SAVOURY TITBITS

Savoury baked goods need to be included in this book. Even though they don't include a lot of sugar, they are usually high in carbohydrates and contain a lot of refined flours, so they have the same effect on our blood sugar levels as foods with a higher sugar content.

SAUSAGE ROLLS

MAKES ABOUT 10

When I was researching lower carb pastry I read a lot about fathead pastry, which is really great and a useful addition to one's baking repertoire. Obviously, it is high in calories (but then so is normal pastry), but it's great for those following a low carb diet and it will not affect your blood sugar levels. Keep in mind that it behaves rather differently to normal pastry too, so practice makes perfect. It is also very rich, so you don't tend to eat as much of it. I love sausage rolls and these are now a firm favourite served with low-sugar ketchup and mustard.

200g grated mozzarella
100g ground almonds
2 tbsp cream cheese
1 egg
1 tsp wholegrain mustard
1 tsp picked thyme leaves
Salt and pepper
4 high meat content and
    gluten-free sausages
(Homemade ketchup and
    mustard to serve)

Preheat the oven to 180C/gas mark 4. Then take the sausages, make an incision down the side of each one and carefully peel off the skins. Lay them on a lined baking sheet and cook for about 8-10 minutes. You want them just cooked (they will cook more later) but not browned. Take them out of the oven and cool.

To make the pastry, layer the mozzarella in the bottom of a non-stick saucepan. Heat slowly to melt, stirring occasionally. Add the cream cheese, mustard and thyme leaves, plus a good pinch of salt and pepper.

Stir until everything comes together. Take off the heat and beat in the almonds and, finally, the egg. Mix well to form a dough and then unload on to a sheet of baking paper. Press down and cover with another sheet of baking paper. Using a rolling pin, roll over the paper until the pastry is about 1/2cm thick.

Take off the top sheet and trim to form a rectangle about 9 inches wide and 4 inches in length, then cut down the middle lengthwise. Place the two sausages across the pastry and roll up, joining the pastry where it comes together. Use the baking paper to assist you and tighten the roll up. Then cut into smaller rolls, place back on the baking sheet and bake for 20 minutes until golden brown. Take out and cool.

CHEESE CRACKERS

Yep, these cheese crackers are made of....well...more cheese! I have to say, in my book this is a good thing; I love cheese! These are great to have with soft cheese or as a savoury nibble. They are also good with sliced apple, if you crave a sweet hit and also want to keep the protein levels up.

200g grated mozzarella
100g ground almonds
2 tbsp cream cheese
1 egg
1 tsp picked thyme leaves
Salt and pepper

To make the pastry, place the mozzarella in a layer on the bottom of a non-stick saucepan. Slowly start to heat up and melt, stirring occasionally. Add the cream cheese and thyme leaves, plus a good amount of salt and pepper. Mix well until all is combined. Take off the heat and beat in the almonds and the egg. Mix well to form a dough and then unload on to a sheet of baking paper. Press down and cover with another sheet of baking paper. Using a rolling pin, roll the pastry between the sheets of paper until thin (about ½ cm).

Take off the top sheet and trim to form a rectangle, and then cut down the middle lengthwise. Next cut this into squares before popping back into the oven and cooking for 10 more minutes. When cooked, take out and cool before serving with soft cheese and apple slices.

PEPPERONI, CHILLI TOMATO AND BASIL PIZZA

MAKES 2

Pizza is one of my favourite dishes EVER and it also happens to normally be off the list of allowed food on my low blood sugar diet. This is quite rich, so I like to use punchy, strong toppings such as olives, capers, spicy salami, red onions and anchovies.

Pastry
200g grated mozzarella
100g ground almonds
2 tbsp cream cheese
1 egg
1 tsp garlic powder
1 tsp dried oregano
Salt and pepper

Topping
150ml passata
1 tub of mini mozzarella balls
150g spicy pepperoni slices
1 tsp chilli flakes
Handful of basil

Simply add the mozzarella in a layer to the bottom of a non-stick saucepan. Slowly start to heat up and melt, stirring occasionally. Add the cream cheese, garlic powder and dried oregano, plus a good pinch of salt and pepper. Mix together until everything is melted, take off the heat and beat in the almonds and the egg. Mix well to form a dough, and unload on to a sheet of baking paper. Press down and then cover with another sheet of baking paper. Using a rolling pin, roll into a large circle or disk, to be your ideal pizza shape. Then let it sit for 10 minutes.

Next heat the oven up to 180C/gas mark 4, then take off the top sheet of paper, place on a baking sheet or pizza stone, and bake for 10 minutes or until golden brown all over. Spoon over some of the passata, pushing to the edges, then spread in the mini mozzarella, salami and chilli. Place back in the oven and cook for 15-20 more minutes. Take out and sprinkle with basil leaves and serve with a green salad.

PARMESAN TARTLETS

MAKES 4 MEDIUM OR 10–15 BITE-SIZED TARTLETS

These are not classic baking, but they are so addictive that I had to include them. They are brilliant for low-carb canapés, for that all-important crunch factor, and are interesting to serve salads in.

300g grated Parmesan cheese

Filling ideas for the larger tarts
Various salad leaves
Sliced steak
Roasted veggies
Spicy chicken strips

Smaller tarts
Whipped goat's cheese and
    pickle
Pan-fried mushrooms,
    mozzarella and pesto
Diced tomato and basil
Caponata

Preheat the oven to 160°C/gas mark 3 and line a baking sheet with greaseproof paper. Sprinkle the cheese in an even layer across the tray. Pop in the oven for 15 minutes, or until melted and golden brown. Then take out, and while still hot, cut out with ring cutters to fit the size you want (say 1½ inches for canapé size, 6 inches for individual tarts). Press into the moulds. I use mini muffin trays for the canapé sized tarts and normal muffin trays for the individual size, and bowls for the large ones for salad.

CHEESE AND BLACK PEPPER TOASTED MUFFINS

MAKES 4

These are slightly more like cake in texture than a normal English muffin as they don't contain gluten, but they are great for breakfast, especially with Eggs Benedict.

200g fine almond meal

2 tbsp coconut flour

2 tsp gluten-free baking
   powder

50g finely grated Parmesan

Salt and lots of black pepper

100g melted butter

4 eggs

Preheat the oven to 180C/gas mark 4. Generously grease four ramekins with softened butter. Mix the almond meal, coconut flour, salt, pepper, baking powder and Parmesan. Then whisk the eggs and melted butter together and mix well into the dry ingredients, place in the ramekins and bake for 10–15 minutes, until golden brown. Take out and cool. When cooled, slice in half then toast and serve with butter. For plain muffins, omit the cheese and black pepper.

SPINACH AND ARTICHOKE CALZONE

SERVES 2

Who doesn't love an oozing cheesy calzone? I have filled this with vegetables, but you can add shredded chicken, ham, tomato, or anything you want really. The key is to experiment. I think it would be good with Mexican spices and ground beef too, so do have a play.

Pastry
200g grated mozzarella (plus 100g, see below)
100g ground almonds
2 tbsp cream cheese
1 egg
1 tsp garlic powder
1 tsp dried oregano
Salt and pepper

Filling
250g spinach leaves
200g tinned or bottled artichoke hearts
50g goats cheese (optional)
100g Fresh mozzarella
1 tsp dried chilli flakes
Sugar-free tomato ketchup from page 83 or warm passata to serve

Simply add the mozzarella in a layer to the bottom of a non-stick saucepan. Slowly start to heat up and melt, stirring occasionally. Add the cream cheese, mustard and thyme leaves, plus a good pinch of salt and pepper. Mix well until everything is combined. Then take off the heat and beat in the almonds and finally the egg. Mix well to form a dough, and then unload on to a sheet of baking paper. Press down and then cover with another sheet of baking paper. Using a rolling pin, roll between the sheets of paper until thin (about ½ cm).

To prepare the filling, heat a touch of olive oil in a frying pan and add the spinach. Cook gently for about 6-8 minutes, until wilted. Drain any liquid off and roughly chop. Cut the artichokes into small pieces and mix with the spinach, chilli and torn mozzarella, and season well.

Preheat the oven to 200C/gas mark 6. Cut the 'pastry' into two large disks, about the width of a small dining plate (roughly 6 inches), and lay on a non-stick baking paper sheet on a baking tray. Add some of the filling to the centre of each one. Then take one side and fold over so the edges join the other. Press together using your fingers to make a fluted edge or use a fork. Bake for 15-20 minutes until golden brown. Serve with the tomato sauce and salad.

CARAMELISED ONION, THYME AND PARMESAN TART

SERVES 8

Slowly caramelised onions with thyme and butter are one of life's best flavours. This is such a hit, yet so easy and budget-friendly too. You can of course add whatever ingredients you have to hand, so it's great for using up leftovers.

Shortcrust pastry
2 eggs
1 tbsp extra virgin olive oil
½ tsp sea salt
120g coconut flour
100g cold butter, cubed

Filling
5 white onions
3 cloves garlic sliced
50g butter
2 whole eggs
3 egg yolks
150ml double cream
2 sprigs fresh thyme
Salt and pepper
50g grated Parmesan

Preheat the oven to 200C/gas mark 6. Add the butter, salt and flour to a mixer, and mix until like breadcrumbs, then whisk the eggs and oil together and add to the mix. Continue mixing until a crumbly dough is formed. Then take out of the mixer and roll out between two sheets of baking paper. Press into a pie or tart dish, spike with a fork and blind bake for 20 minutes. While that is cooking you can make the filling. Peel and finely slice the onions and garlic, then cook on a low heat for 30 minutes, with the thyme, seasoning and butter until golden brown and sweet.

Take off the heat and cool. Whisk the eggs, egg yolks, double cream, salt and pepper together. Now you can assemble the tart. Spread the onion mix on the bottom of the tart case, pour over the egg mix and sprinkle with grated Parmesan. Turn the oven down to 150C/gas mark 2 and cook for 40 minutes or until the tart is set and golden brown. Take out of the oven, cool slightly and then serve with a green salad.

EXTRAS

This chapter has a few of those 'extras' that always seem harmless enough, but actually contain masses of sugar. Hopefully it will give you the tools to build up a larder of healthier sauces and spreads.

SUGAR-FREE BBQ SAUCE

MAKES 500ML

My guilty secret is that I love condiments, especially ketchup and BBQ sauce. I can add them to just about everything, and although they taste good, the shop-brought ones tend to be packed with sugar. You will see there is a slightly random ingredient, smoke extract, used here. If you like making BBQ sauce and enjoy this recipe then I recommend you get some, as it does add a depth of flavour and that all-important smokiness. You can also add it to mashed potato, stews and rice dishes, and it comes in various flavours, from Hickory Smoke to Maplewood. I buy mine on Amazon or from MSK Ingredients in the UK.

400g tomato puree
300ml cider vinegar
200g *Xylitol*
1 tsp English mustard
1 tbsp Worcestershire sauce
1 tsp smoked paprika
½ tsp garlic powder
½ tsp celery salt
Pinch of ground cloves
Pinch of cinnamon
Pinch of white pepper
½ tsp of smoke extract
  (optional)
1 tsp salt

Add all the ingredients to a medium saucepan. Bring to the boil, then turn down and simmer for 30 minutes until thick and glossy. Cool and keep in an airtight jar. Keeps for a few weeks in the fridge.

SUGAR-FREE TOMATO KETCHUP

MAKES 500ML

This tastes great with so many recipes, especially the calzone and sausage rolls, and I keep some in my fridge at all times. You can even add chilli to give it a kick.

400g tomato puree
200ml cider vinegar
150g *Xylitol*
1 tsp English mustard
1 tbsp Worchester sauce
½ tsp garlic powder
1 tsp onion powder
½ tsp celery salt
Pinch of ground cloves
Pinch of cinnamon
Pinch of white pepper
2 tsp salt

Add all the ingredients to a medium saucepan. Bring to the boil, then turn down the heat and simmer for 30 minutes until thick and glossy. Cool and keep in an airtight jar. Keeps for a few weeks in the fridge.

MUSTARD

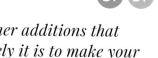

Most mustards contain gluten, sugar and various other additions that aren't really needed. I can't begin to tell you how lovely it is to make your own mustard, and how easy it is. You can blend it for a smooth texture, but personally, I love the wholegrains. This is my basic recipe but you can add so much more, such as grated horseradish, chilli flakes, maple syrup, spices – the list is endless, and it keeps for weeks in the fridge.

200g yellow mustard seeds
100g brown mustard seeds
500ml apple cider vinegar
1 tbsp honey (optional)

Simply mix all the ingredients except for the honey and leave them to sit overnight. The mustard seeds will soak up all the vinegar. Then take half of the mix and blitz until smooth, then add to the remaining mix. Finally, season and add the honey (if you need or want to be really strict then miss this out).

RASPBERRY JAM & STRAWBERRY JAM

MAKES 500ML APPROXIMATELY

I experimented with two types of jam recipes. If you don't want to use pectin as a thickener and you want to enjoy the health benefits of chia seeds, then they do thicken the jam slightly. For a more classic jam recipe use the one below.

400g raspberries
100g *Xylitol*
50g chia seeds
Juice of ½ lemon
1 tsp vanilla

Pop all the ingredients in a heavy based saucepan and bring to the boil, then turn down and simmer for 20-30 minutes on a low heat. Skim off any foam that rises to the surface, take off the heat when ready, cool and pour into sterilised jars. Because it doesn't have the usual preservative properties of jam that is made with sugar, it is best kept in the fridge.

1kg raspberries
250g *Xylitol*
2 tsp pectin
1 tsp vanilla

Pop all the ingredients in a heavy based saucepan and bring to the boil, then turn down and simmer for 40-60 minutes on a low heat. Skim off any foam that rises to the surface. Take off the heat when ready, cool and pour into sterilised jars. As above, this is best kept in the fridge.

STRABERRY CHIA JAM

400g strawberries, halved
100g *Xylitol*
50g chia seeds
Juice of ½ lemon
1 tsp vanilla

Or

500g strawberries
150g *Xylitol*
1 large tsp pectin
1 tsp lemon juice
1 tsp vanilla

Pop all the ingredients into heavy based saucepan and bring to the boil, then turn down and simmer for 20-30 minutes on a low heat. Skim off any foam that rises to the surface. Take off the heat when ready, cool and pour into sterilised jars. Again, be sure to keep this in the fridge.

Pop all the ingredients in a heavy based saucepan and bring to the boil, then turn down and simmer for 40-60 minutes on a low heat. Skim off any foam that rises to the surface. Take off the heat when ready, cool and pour into sterilised jars. Refrigerate.

FRUIT CURDS

MAKES 500ML

These are lovely to have in the fridge and they are great with pancakes, on hot toast, with yoghurt or meringues, cakes and muffins – they really are very versatile. They also taste just as good without sugar, so I always like to have a pot in the fridge, and I change the flavours according to the time of year. Raspberry and blood orange are also good.

LEMON CURD

MAKES 300–400ML

5 unwaxed lemons (zest of 3 and juice
    of all)
250g *Xylitol*
Pinch of salt
100g butter

Mix the juice, zest, *Xylitol,* salt and eggs together well. Then pour into a medium, non-stick saucepan and gently start to cook on a low heat. You need to constantly stir it to stop it from curdling, it should take about 8/10 minutes. Then add the butter, stir until melted and take off the heat. You can then pour into sterilised jars. I keep mine in the fridge and it's good for a week.

PASSIONFRUIT CURD

MAKES 300–400ML

10 passion fruit
4 eggs
1 lime, zest and juice
250g *Xylitol*
Pinch of salt
100g butter

Firstly take the passionfruit juice and seeds out of the fruit and into a bowl. Mix the juice of the passionfruit, lime zest and juice, *Xylitol,* salt and eggs together well. Then pour into a medium, non-stick saucepan and gently start to cook on a low heat. You need to constantly stir it to stop it from curdling, it should take about 8/10 minutes. The add the butter, stir until melted and take off the heat. You can then pour into sterilised jars. I keep mine in the fridge and it's good for a week.

SHORTCRUST PASTRY

MAKES ENOUGH FOR A LARGE TART

OK, so this doesn't act EXACTLY like normal pastry; it's very 'short' and crumbly, so you need to press it into the tin. It will fall apart, as it has no stretchy gluten, but just mould it back when you need it. It can be pressed back in easily and will bake into its shape. Hang in there and it will be your new friend.

2 eggs
1 tbsp extra virgin olive oil
½ tsp sea salt
120g coconut flour
100g cold butter cubed

Preheat the oven to 200C/gas mark 6. Add the butter, salt and flour to a mixer, and mix until it looks like breadcrumbs. Whisk the eggs and oil together and add to the mix. Continue mixing until a crumbly dough is formed. Then take out of the mixer and roll out between two sheets of baking paper. Press into a pie or tart dish, prick with a fork and blind bake for 20 minutes. This is good for sweet and savoury tarts, and classic baking.

CHOCOLATE SHORTCRUST PASTRY

3 eggs
1 tbsp coconut oil
½ tsp sea salt
50g cocoa powder
120g coconut flour
125g cold butter, cubed
½ tsp Vanilla extract
50g *Xylitol*

Preheat the oven to 200C/gas mark 6 and follow the above recipe, but don't forget to add the additional ingredients.

FATHEAD PASTRY

200g grated mozzarella
100g ground almonds
2 tbsp cream cheese
1 egg
Salt and pepper

Layer the mozzarella on the bottom of a non-stick saucepan. Slowly start to heat up and melt, stirring occasionally. Add the cream cheese, plus a good pinch of salt and pepper. Mix until melted and combined in one mass. Then take off the heat and beat in the almonds and finally the egg. Mix well to form a dough and then unload on to a sheet of baking paper. Press down and then cover with another sheet of baking paper. This can be used for pizza, sausage rolls, flatbreads, cheese sticks, crackers, rolls and calzone.

ICE CREAMS

Ice creams lend themselves well to low-sugar versions. The chocolate recipe here is one of the best chocolate ice creams I have ever made and you can use the vanilla as a base for more flavours. You do need a proper ice cream machine though; I use my Cuisinart one. All of these mixes can also be poured into lolly moulds and served as an ice lolly as well.

VANILLA ICE CREAM

500ml double cream
200ml milk
4 egg yolks
150g *Xylitol*
1 vanilla pod scraped of seeds
Pinch of sea salt

This is the basic recipe I use. Start by simply heating the milk, cream, vanilla pod and seeds in a saucepan. Then whisk the eggs and the *Xylitol* in a bowl. When the milk mix is just coming to the boil, pour it over the egg yolks and *Xylitol* and whisk, and then pour it all back into the saucepan and gently heat for about 5 minutes. Do not boil as it will curdle; you just want to thicken it slightly. Take it off the heat, cool and pour into the ice cream machine, and churn in the usual way.

CHOCOLATE ICE CREAM

450ml double cream
150ml milk
300g dark chocolate
    (70% cocoa solids and finely
    chopped)
5 egg yolks
100g *Xylitol*
½ tsp sea salt

Heat the double cream in a saucepan until just boiling, then take off the heat and add the chocolate, stirring until melted. Whisk the egg yolks together with the *Xylitol*, until slightly paler. Heat the milk in a separate saucepan and then pour over the egg mix, stir well and pop back in the pan, and heat gently for about 5 minutes until it looks slightly thicker. Then stir into the chocolate mix. Cool completely, then add to the ice cream machine, churn for 60 minutes and transfer into a container to chill in the freezer for a few hours. Serve with a shot of espresso poured over the top and amaretti biscuits for a dinner party dessert.

HONEY AND SEA SALT ICE CREAM

500ml double cream
200ml milk
5 egg yolks
200ml runny honey
2 tsp sea salt flakes

I love making this mix into ice lollies then dipping them in dark chocolate. Simply heat the milk, cream and salt in a saucepan. Then whisk the egg yolks and the honey in a bowl. When the milk mix is just coming to the boil, pour it over the egg mix and whisk, then pour it all back into the saucepan and gently heat for about 5 minutes. Do not boil as it will curdle; you just want to thicken it slightly. Take it off the heat, cool and pour into the ice cream machine and churn in the usual way.

LIME AND COCONUT ICE CREAM

600ml coconut milk
200ml double cream
5 egg yolks
100g *Xylitol* (or coconut sugar
    if you don't have to be uber
    strict)
Zest of 2 limes
1 shot Malibu or coconut
    liquor
Pinch of salt

Simply heat the coconut milk, cream and salt in a saucepan. Then whisk the eggs, *Xylitol* and lime zest in a bowl. When the milk mix is just coming to the boil, pour it over the egg mix and whisk, then pour it all back into the saucepan and gently heat for about 5 minutes. Do not boil as it will curdle; you just want to thicken it slightly. Add the Malibu, take it off the heat, cool and then pour into the ice cream machine and churn.

ICE LOLLIES

MAKES 6

An ice lolly can really be helpful when you want a sweet hit quickly. I always have some in the freezer and it stops me grabbing a processed dessert or sweet. Also they are great for kids. You will see a little shot of alcohol in some of them; this can be fun for an after-dinner summer evening for adults and also the alcohol stops the ice crystals from freezing.

GREEK YOGURT HONEY AND SUMMER FRUIT LOLLIES

350ml Greek yoghurt
1 tbsp runny honey
2 drops of *Stevia*
150g of mixed berries (frozen is fine)

This is really simple. Just pop all of the ingredients into a blender, blitz until the berries are semi-crushed and then pour into the mould and freeze!

PINA COLADA LOLLIES

200g pineapple chunks
200ml coconut milk
Zest of one lime
2 drops *Stevia*
2 shots Malibu (optional)

Blitz the pineapple, coconut, *Xylitol* and Malibu together (if using), then stir in the lime zest. Pour into the moulds and freeze.

FRAPPE LOLLIES

250ml milk
100ml double cream
2 tsp good quality espresso
    powder
2 drops *Stevia*
1 tsp vanilla extract
Pinch of salt

Blitz all the ingredients together, then pour into the moulds and freeze.

CLEMENTINE LEMON & SOUR CREAM LOLLIES

300ml sour cream
1 tsp zest of one lemon and one
    clementine
100ml juice from the lemon
100ml clementine juice
3 drops *Stevia*

Mix together, pour into the mould and freeze.

GLOSSARY OF INGREDIENTS AND USEFUL NOTES

Glycemic Index Content (GI Content)

This is how quickly an ingredient turns into sugar (or insulin) in your bloodstream. The lower the GI content the slower it turns into insulin and the longer it takes to release energy to your body. A lower GI is always a healthier option, particularly for people with diabetes and for those who want to maintain a healthy lifestyle and weight.

Xylitol*

This is my go-to sweetener; it's easy to use and I buy it in bulk online through Amazon. It has been tested extensively and is fine to consume on a daily basis if necessary. There is also evidence to suggest that it reduces tooth cavities and it has a GI of 7% instead of pure sugar (glucose), which has a GI of 100%. Finally, it only has 40% of the calories of sugar. In most supermarkets, you can also buy it under the brand name *Total Sweet* and *Truvia*.

Swerve

This is a sweetener that I really like using and you can get great brown sugar and icing sugar versions too. It is more common in the US so I highly recommend it for my American readers, but again, it can be found on Amazon. It comes in slightly pricier for us in the UK, but I am sure it is only a matter of time before it is sold over here.

Stevia

Stevia is very strong and very bitter, which is why it is generally sold in small bottles of liquid. It can be useful though and I always have some for cups of tea and smoothies if they need a sweet boost for my guests.

*Please be aware that *Xylitol* is toxic to dogs.

Erythritol

This is similar to *Xylitol*, though it has fewer calories; in fact is has almost zero calories. It tends to be what I use if I can't get *Xylitol*, as it has a slightly strange cooling effect and mouth feel sometimes (down to its chemical makeup). It won't spike your blood sugars and can be bought online too.

Coconut Oil

This is currently very popular amongst health enthusiasts. It is actually a saturated fat that acts like an unsaturated one in terms of how it behaves healthwise. I love using it for Asian and Caribbean inspired cooking, but it can also add great flavour to baking. It is available is most supermarkets.

Dark Chocolate

I understand that all chocolate (unless its 100% cocoa solids) has sugar in. But it also contains antioxidants and has other health benefits, and I think it's a fantastic ingredient to use. If you use chocolate with a minimum of 70% cocoa solids it adds serious flavour and doesn't upset the blood sugars too much. Plus, it makes you happy!

Nut Butters

These are great binding agents for flour-free baking. I apologise to those with nut allergies; I can't be everything to everyone and next time I will try to write a recipe book that is nut-free too, but I am not there yet. I use cashew nut butter for a neutral base, then peanut and almond for certain dishes.

Ground Almonds/ Almond Flour

You will see almond flour mentioned in various places when you start researching flour-free baking. It is basically ground almonds. You can get different grades though. The chocolate chip cookies, for example, use normal grade and if made with the super fine almond flour, they are not as good, so experiment. The fine almond flour would be good with the muffins.

Coconut Flour

When I first started to experiment, I used to replace normal flour with the same amount of coconut flour. Boy, was that a mistake! I also used to call coconut flour the devil's flour, as it sucks moisture out of bakes like nothing else. I now love it and it actually makes great shortbreads and pastry, down to it being a good, dry product. One tip though – you just never need as much as you think.

Buckwheat Flour

Buckwheat is actually wheat-and gluten-free and comes from a berry, not a grain. It's been used for years in many cultures and it makes the classic French galettes and Russian blinis. I love the flavour and crêpes served with cinnamon-roasted apples and Greek yoghurt is an easy and lovely dessert.

Spelt Flour

This is my favourite flour to use for all my baking and white flour needs. I make fantastic white sauces with it, breads, pancakes, pasta, cakes and biscuits. It is not gluten-free, but it is tolerable for most people with wheat allergies. It also has a lower GI than normal refined flours and is better for your gut. I swear by Sharpham Park products in the UK and Bob's Red Mill in the US.

MEASUREMENTS

As there are a wide range of recipes included in this book, I thought it would be useful to include the measurement conversions as everyone seems to have their favourites they like to work with.

British	American
8oz (225g) butter	1 cup (or two sticks)
1lb (450g) butter	2 cups (or four sticks)
4.5oz (125g) flour	1 cup
7.6oz (215g) *Xylitol*	1 cup
6.3oz (180g) *Swerve*	1 cup
3.5oz (100g) Cocoa Powder	1 cup
4.2oz (120g) Cream Cheese	1 cup
5oz (140g) Oats	1 cup
3.5oz (100g) Dessicated Coconut	1 cup
4oz (110g) Ground Almonds	1 cup
3.5oz(100g) Pistachios	1 cup
5.3oz (150g) Mixed berries	1 cup
6.2oz (175g) Chocolate chips	1 cup
4oz (110g) Grated cheese	1 cup
6.3oz (180g) Chocolate	1 cup
4.5oz (125g) Macadamia Nuts	1 cup
6.2 oz (175g) Dates	1 cup
0.8 oz (23g) Sweetener	1 cup
5.6oz (160g) Chia Seeds	1 cup
7oz (200g) Mustard Seeds	1 cup
9.25oz (266g) Peanut Butter	1 cup
8.5oz (240g) Double Cream	1 cup

Spoons and Cups	ml
¼ tsp	1.25ml
½ tsp	2.5ml
1 tsp	5ml
1 dessert spoon	10ml
1 tbsp	15ml
1 shot	25ml
¼ cup	60ml
1/3 cup	80ml
½ cup	125ml
1 cup	250ml
2 cups	475ml
3 cups	710ml

Gas Mark	°C	°F
1	140°C	275°F
2	150°C	300°F
3	160°C	325°F
4	180°C	350°F
5	190°C	375°F
6	200°C	400°F
7	220°C	425°F
8	230°C	450°F
9	240°C	475°F

All cooking times are based on conventional ovens. For fan assisted ovens, please consult your cooker's manual.

British	American
British	**American**
Double cream	Heavy cream
Bicarbonate of soda	Baking soda
Dark chocolate	Bittersweet chocolate
Soured cream	Sour cream
Cling film	Plastic wrap
Baking paper	Wax paper
Frying pan	Skillet
Grilling	Broiling